Color Me Hawaii

A Tropical Coloring Book For Adventurous Souls Who Want To See Beyond The Horizon.

F. Scott Crawford

Color Me Hawaii

A Tropical Coloring Book For Adventurous Souls Who Want To See Beyond The Horizon.

F. Scott Crawford

Published by:

Black Rock Publishing
3661 Stockton Drive
Carrollton, Texas 75010

Produced in the United States of America.

ISBN-10: 1-51482-552-X
ISBN-13: 978-1514825525

DEDICATION:

For Maggie: "Forever & forever."

WELCOME TO YOUR OWN COLORFUL ISLAND WORLD:

Use the colors that seem best to you.

"Stay in the lines" except when you have to go outside the lines to satisfy your artistic instincts and expand your horizons.

Relax. Concentrate. Use your feelings. Enjoy your creative impulses.

Make a splash. Find the flowers. Surfs up. Sunset makes it spectacular.

Note: The first two drawings have some items in solid black, for your reference and for ideas as to how the original illustrations were set up. The same two drawings are again on the last working pages of your "Color Me Hawaii" coloring book, without the solid black, so you can shade or color them however you desire.

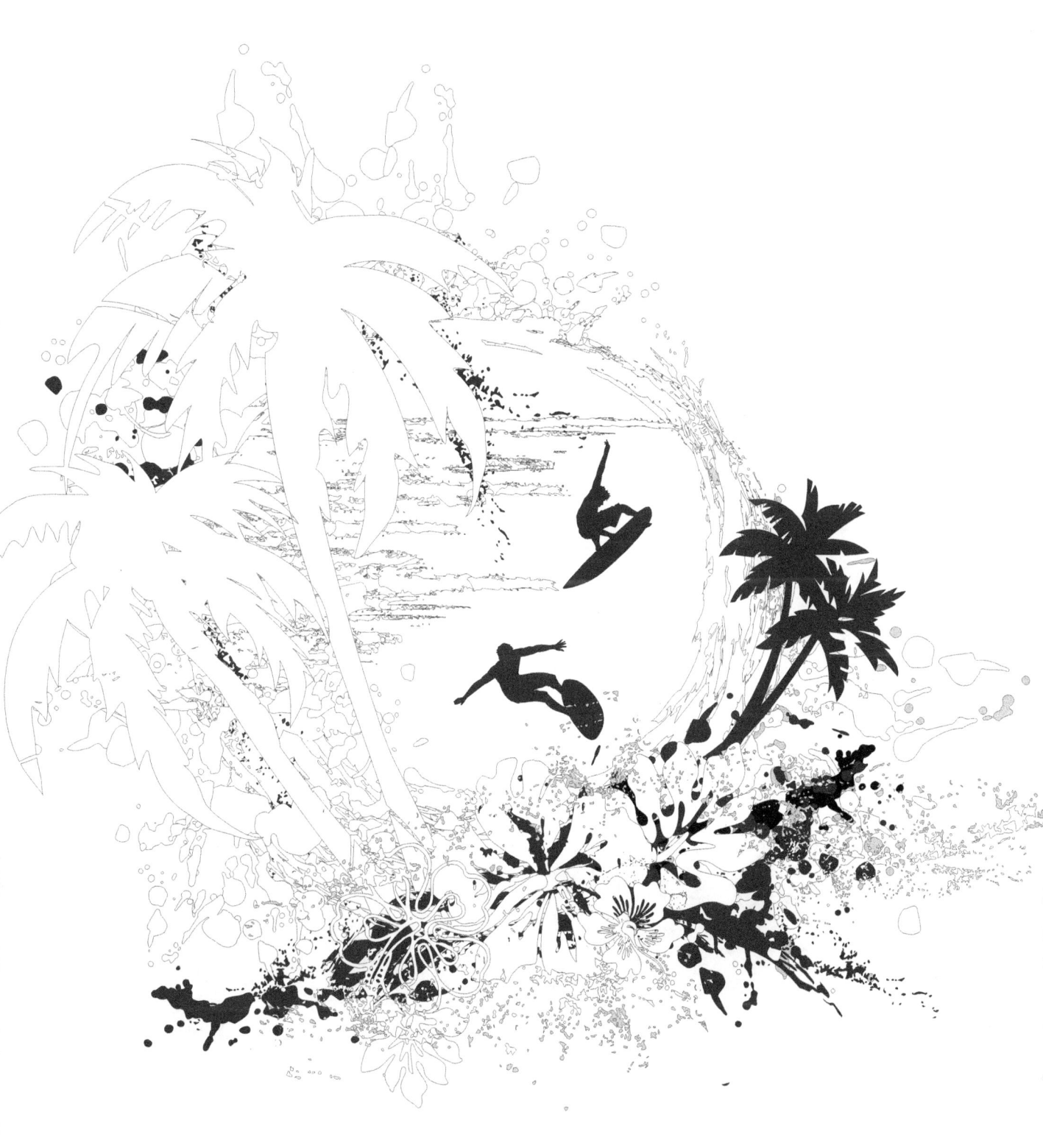

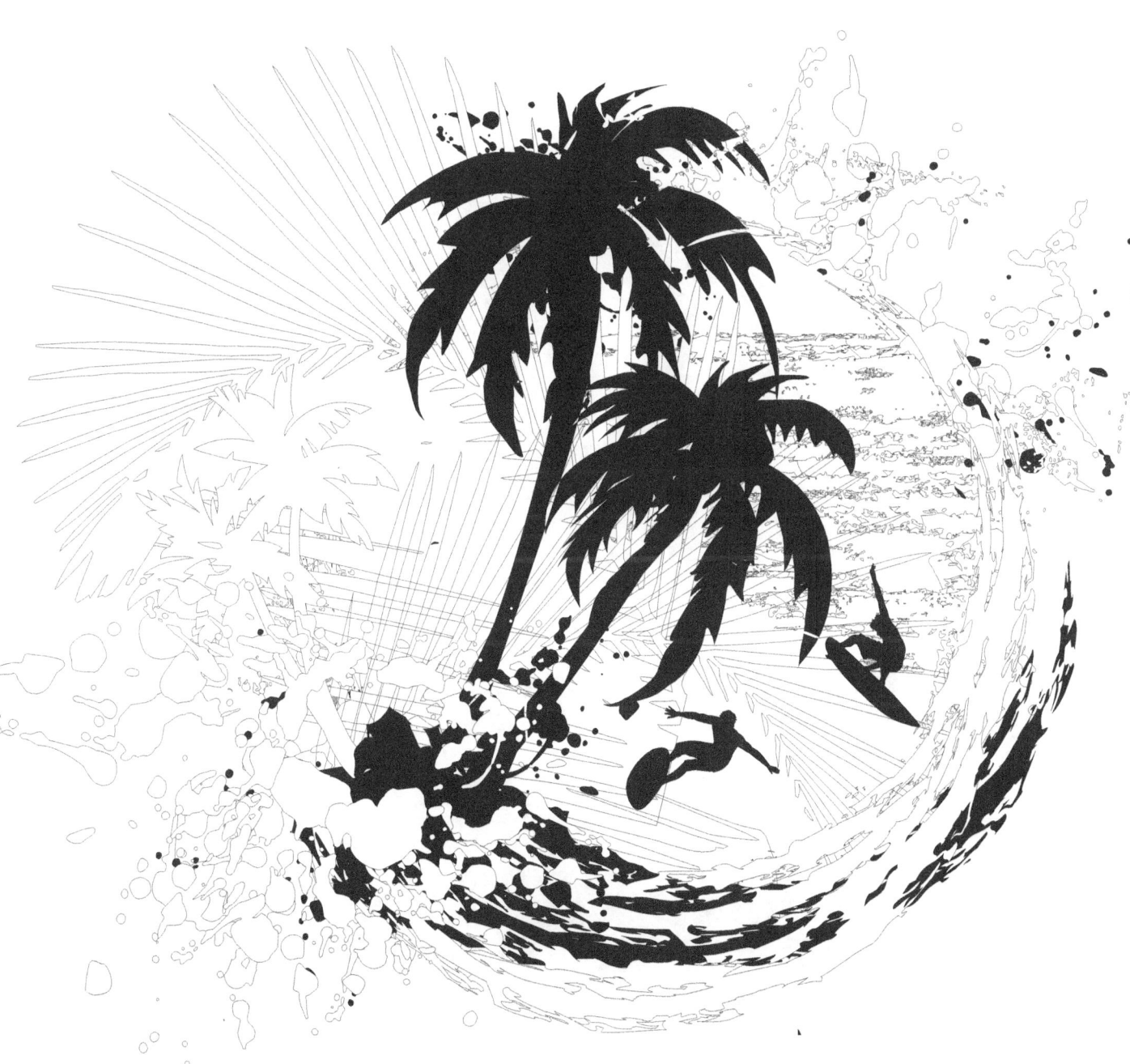

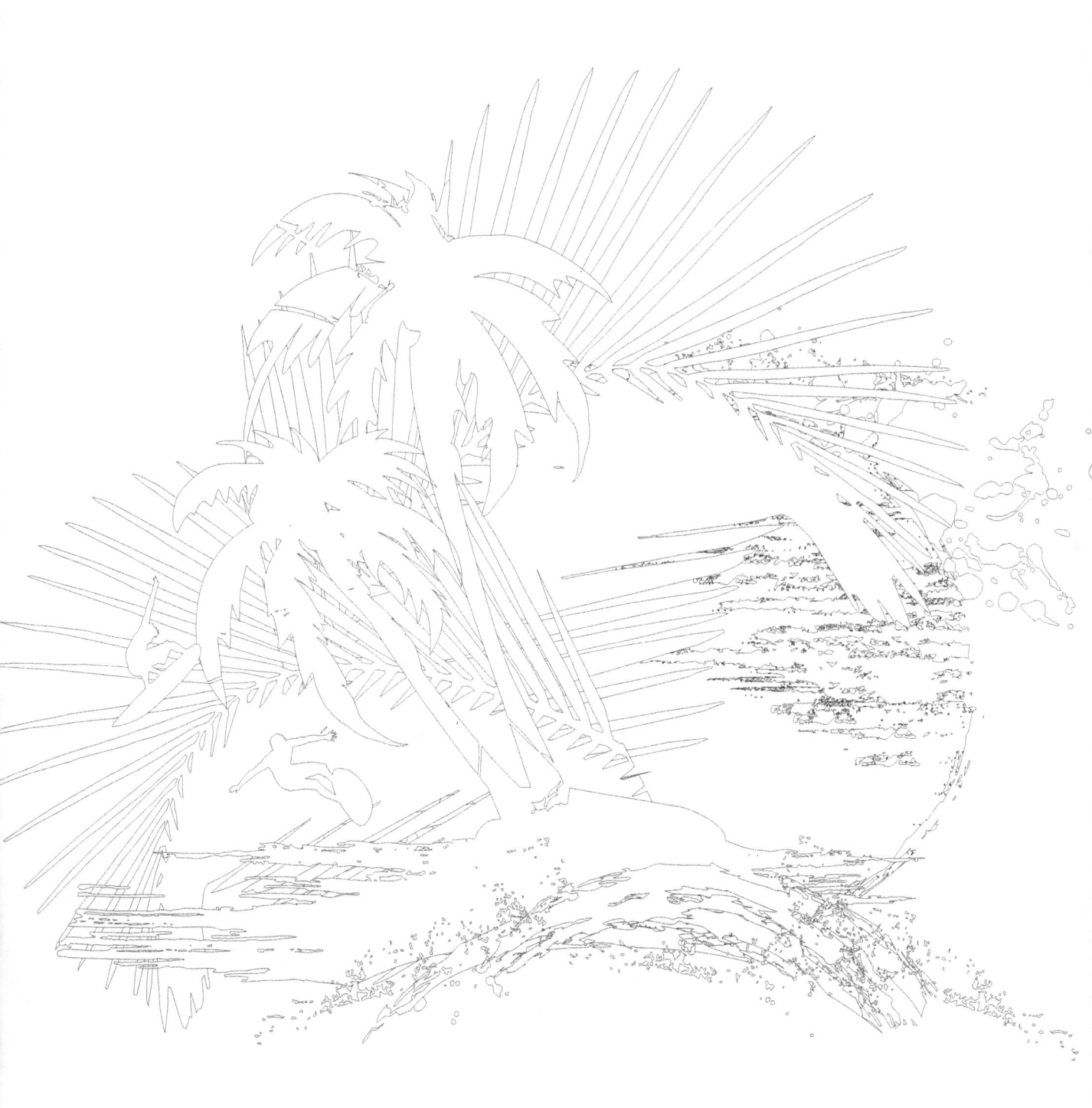

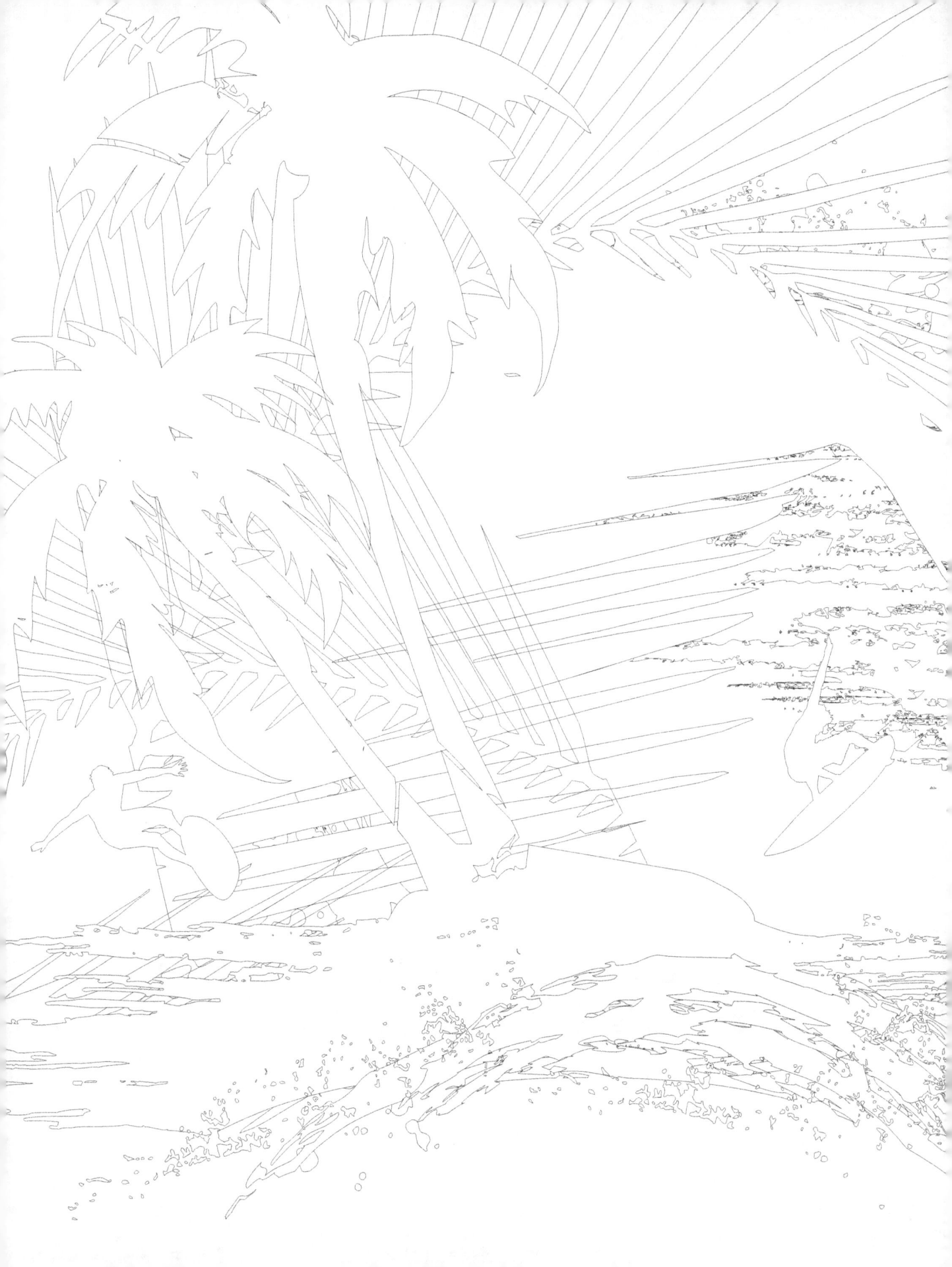

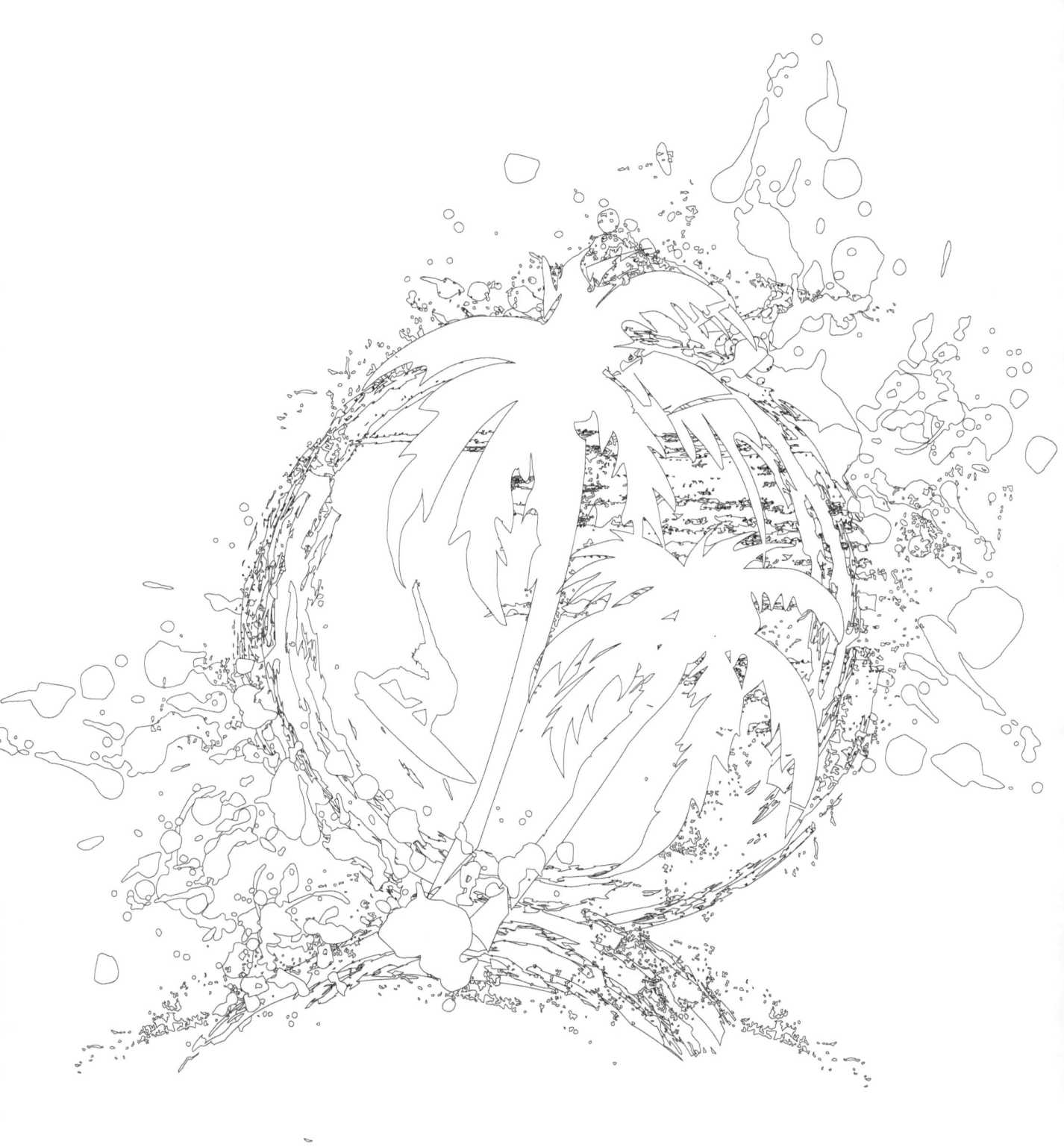

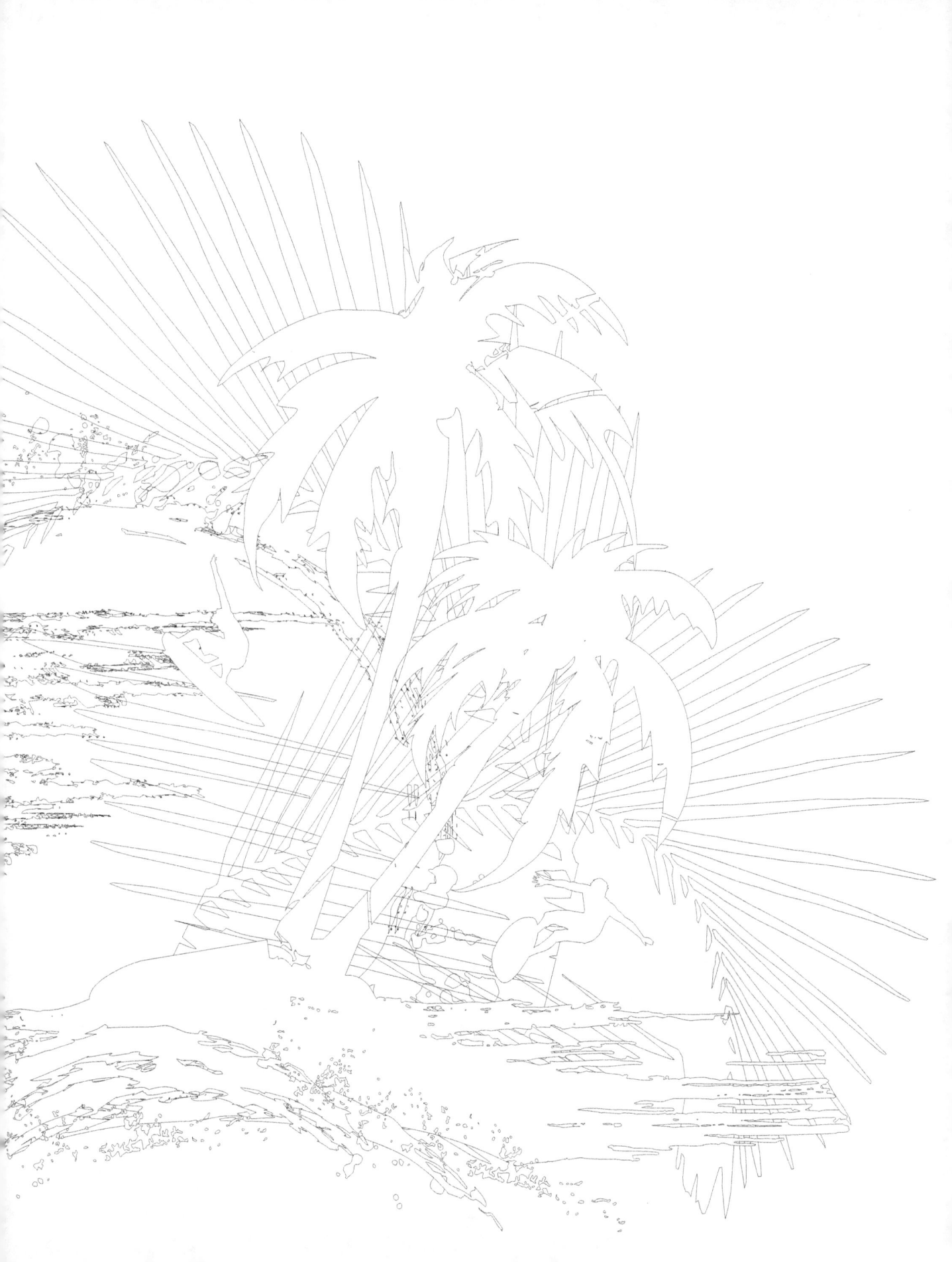

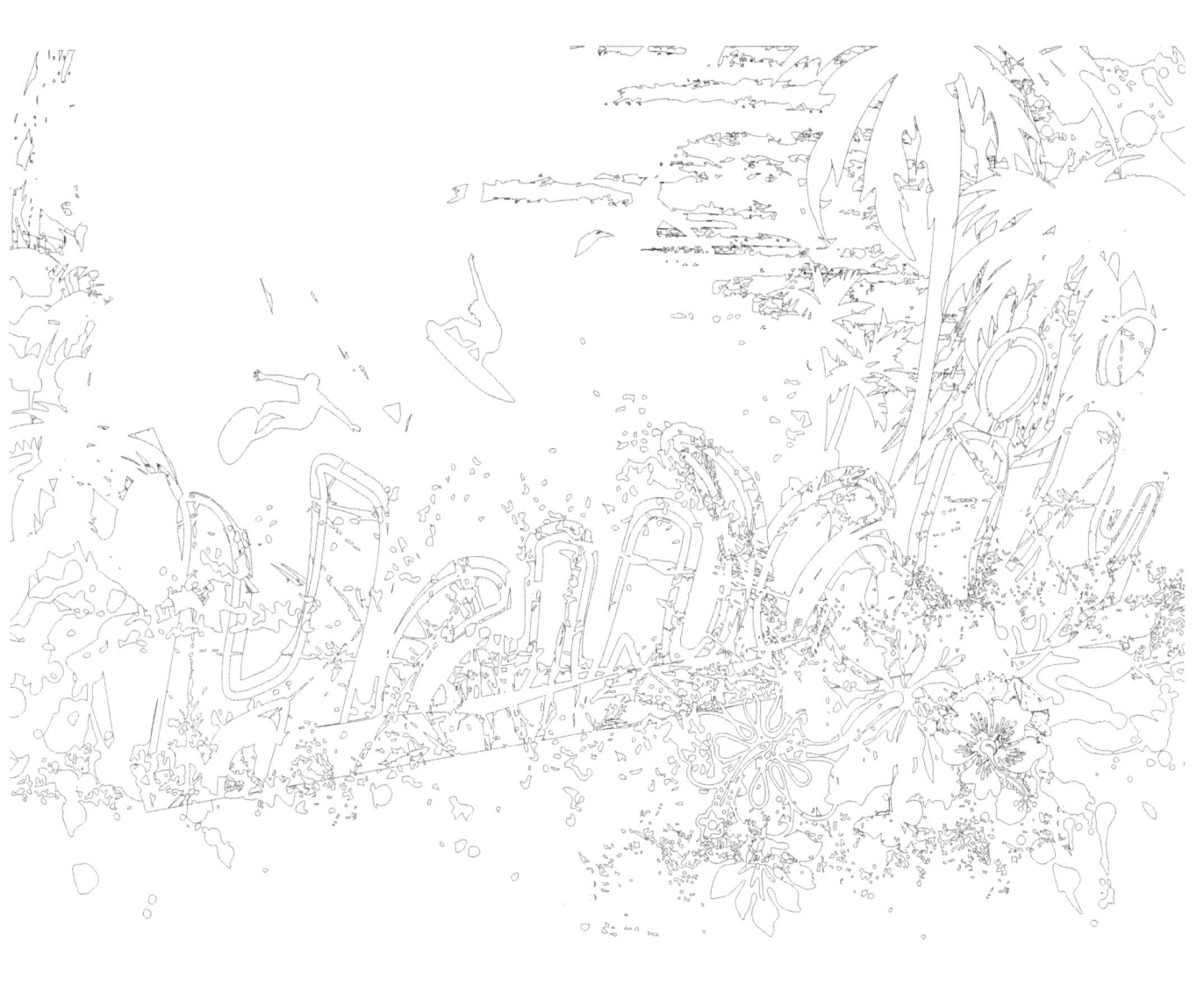

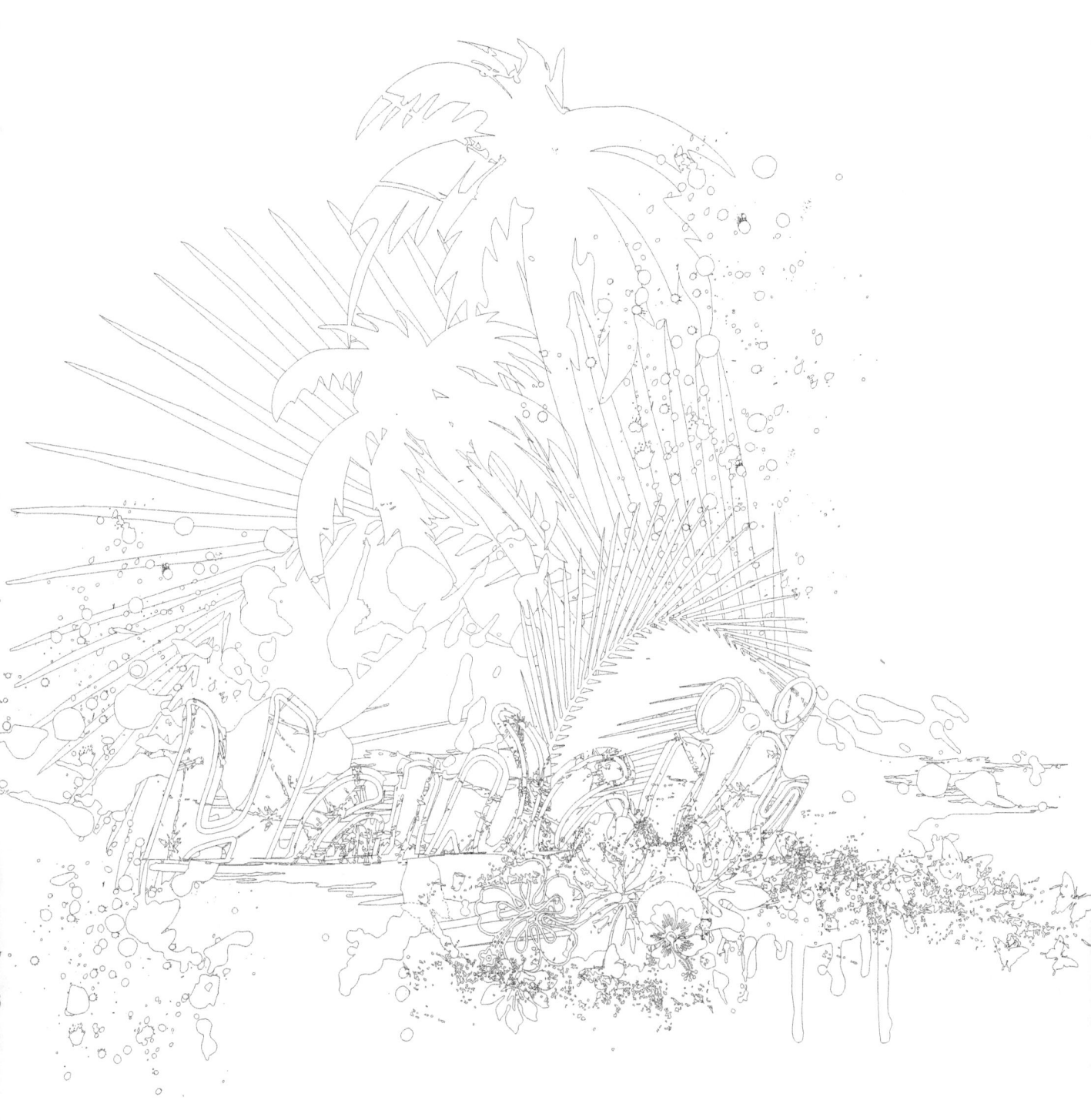

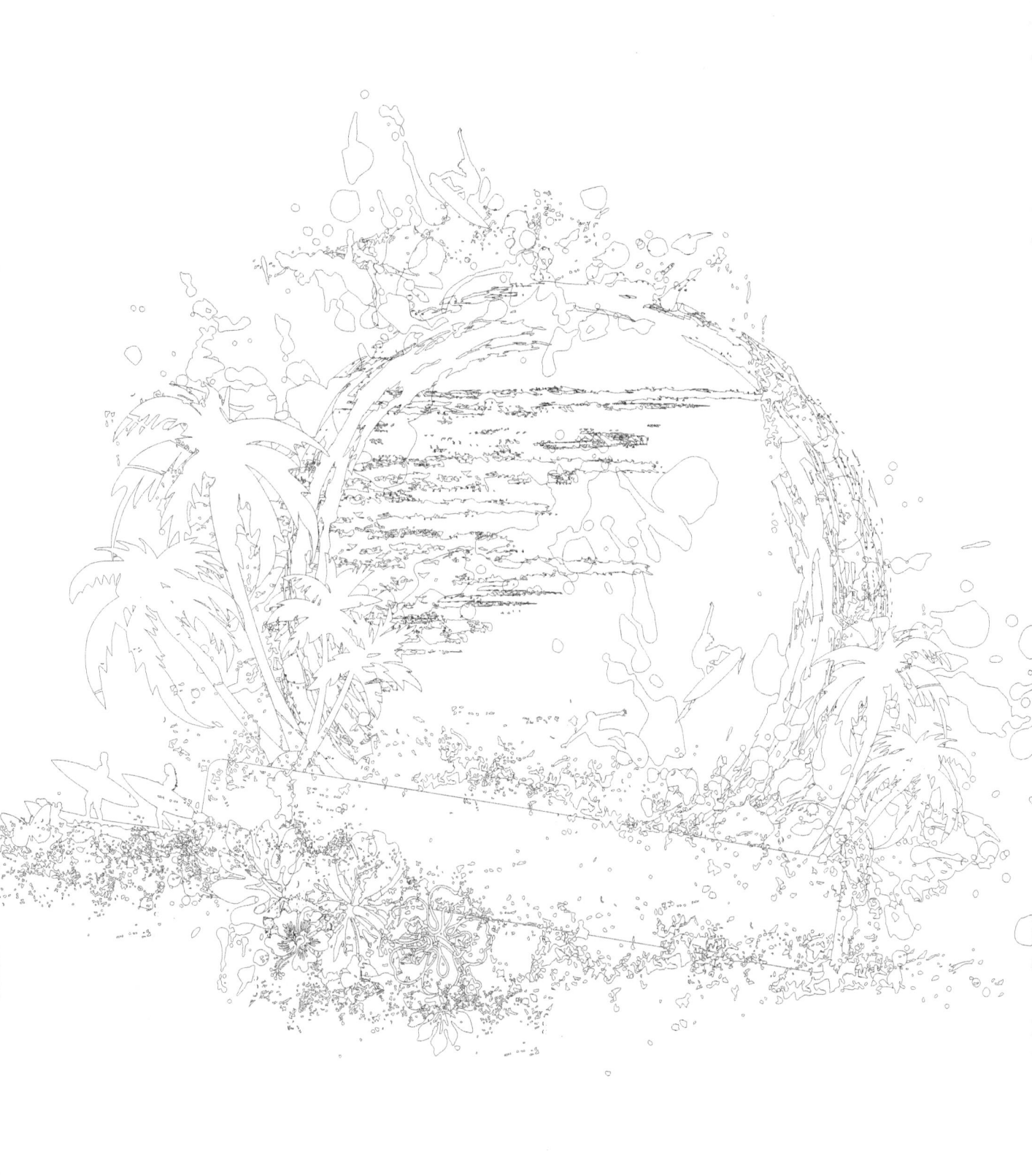

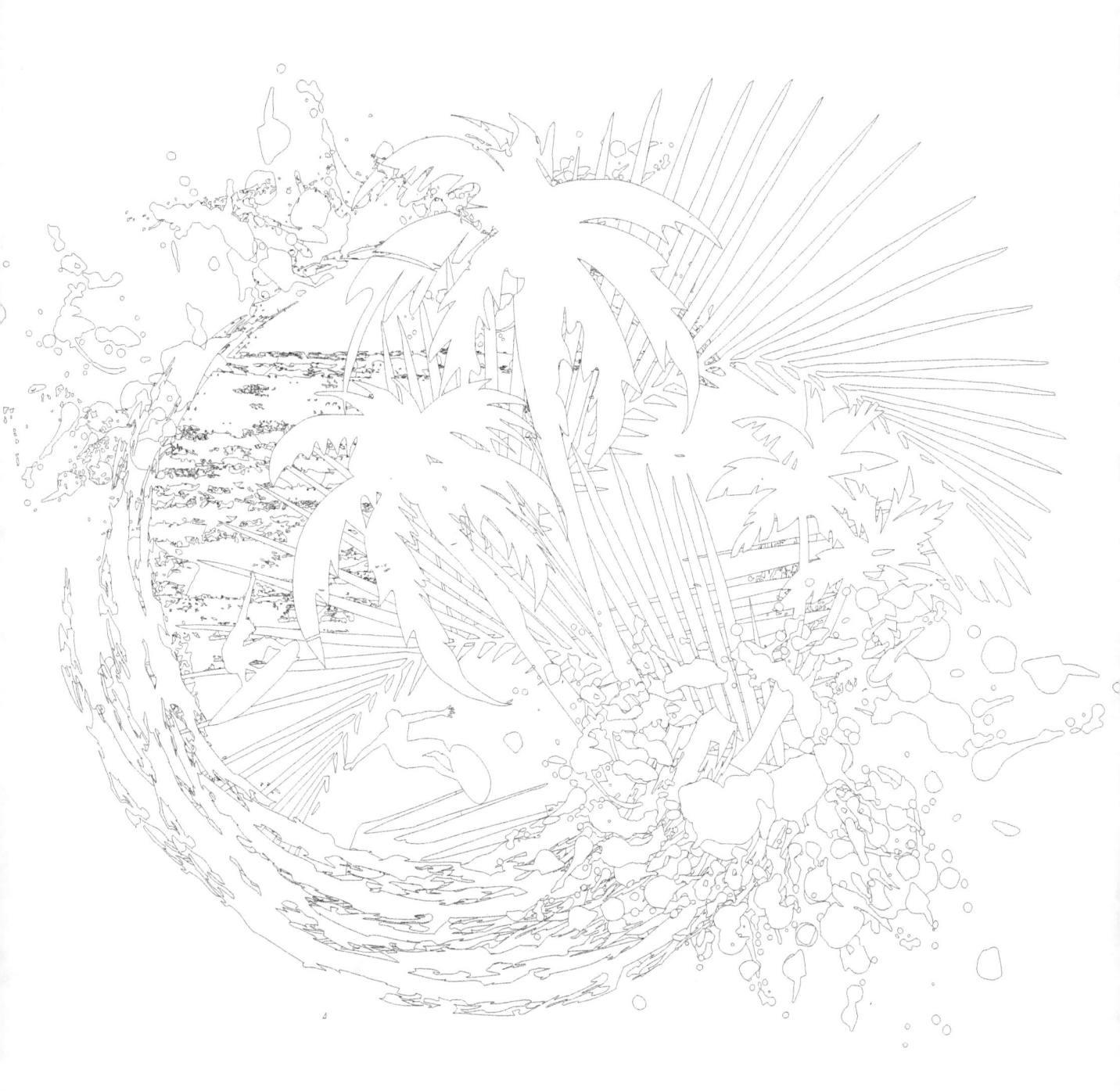

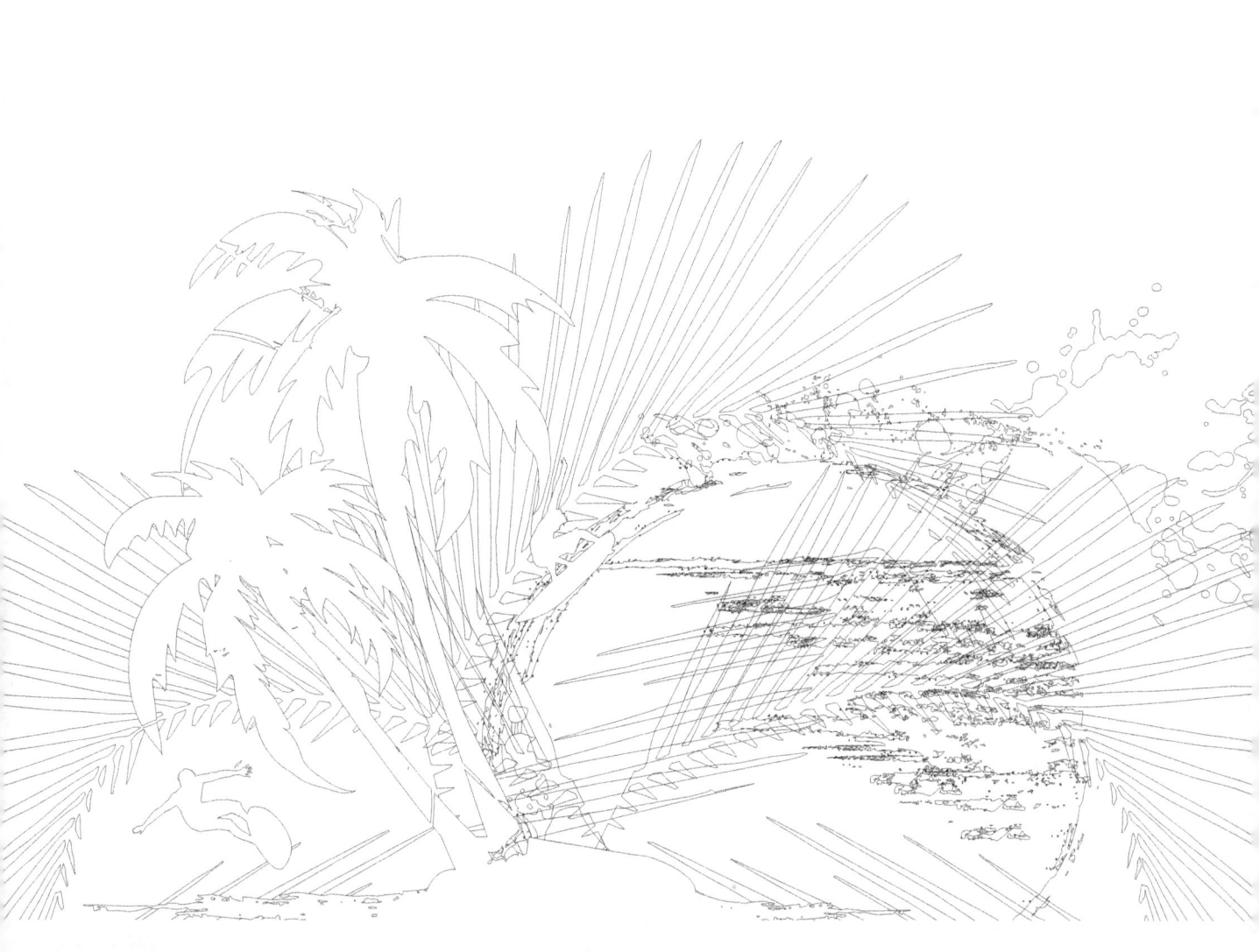

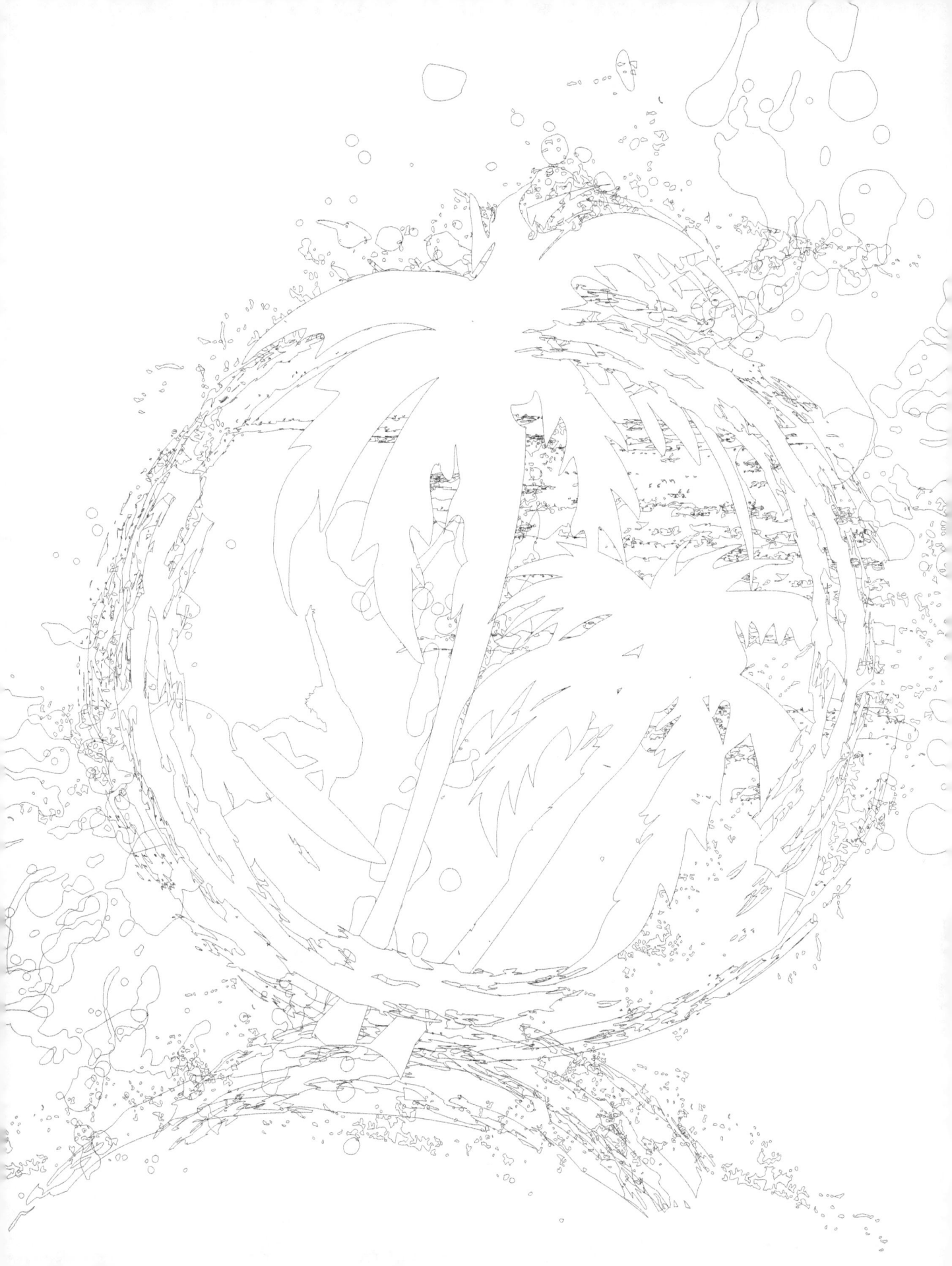

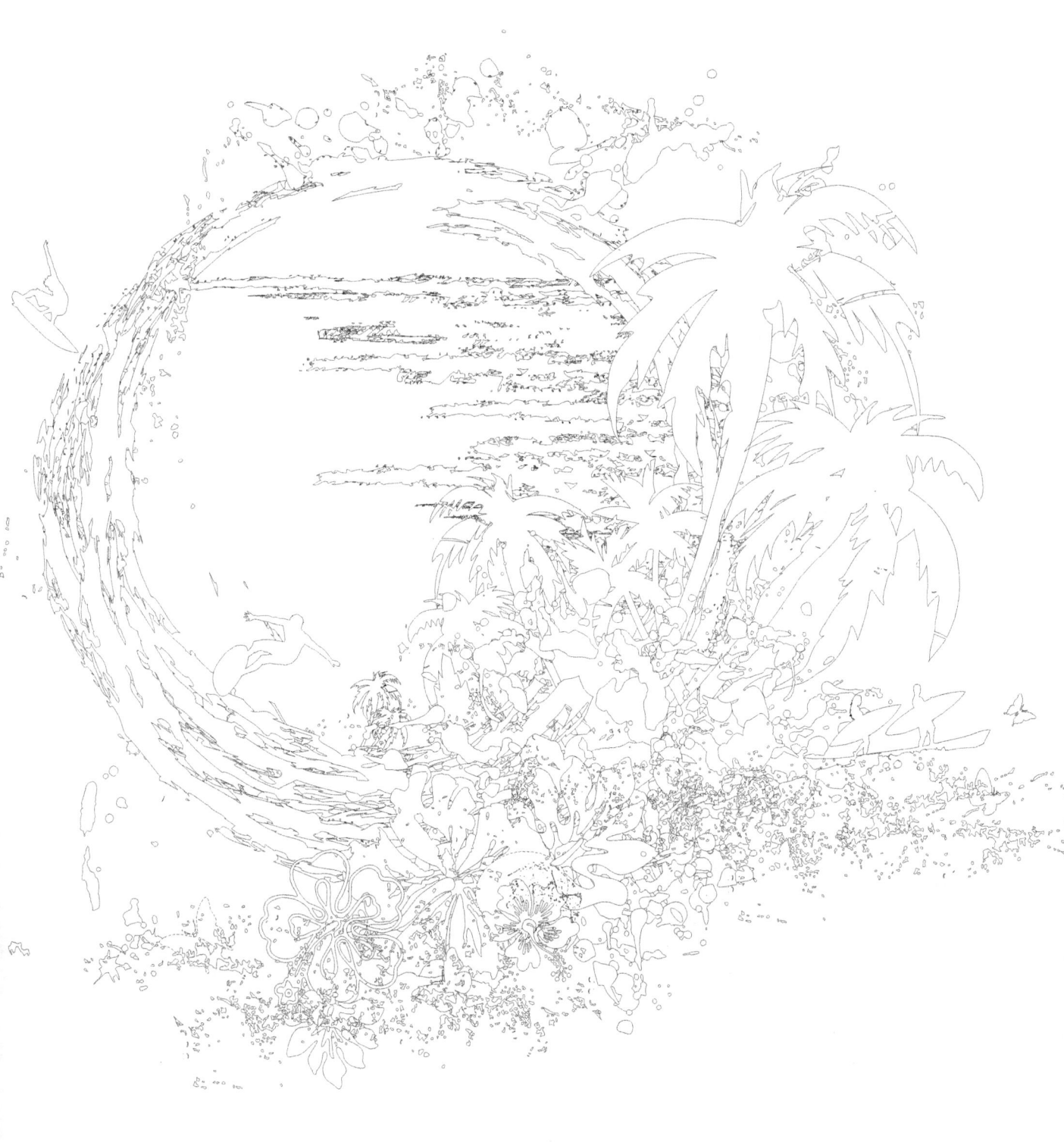

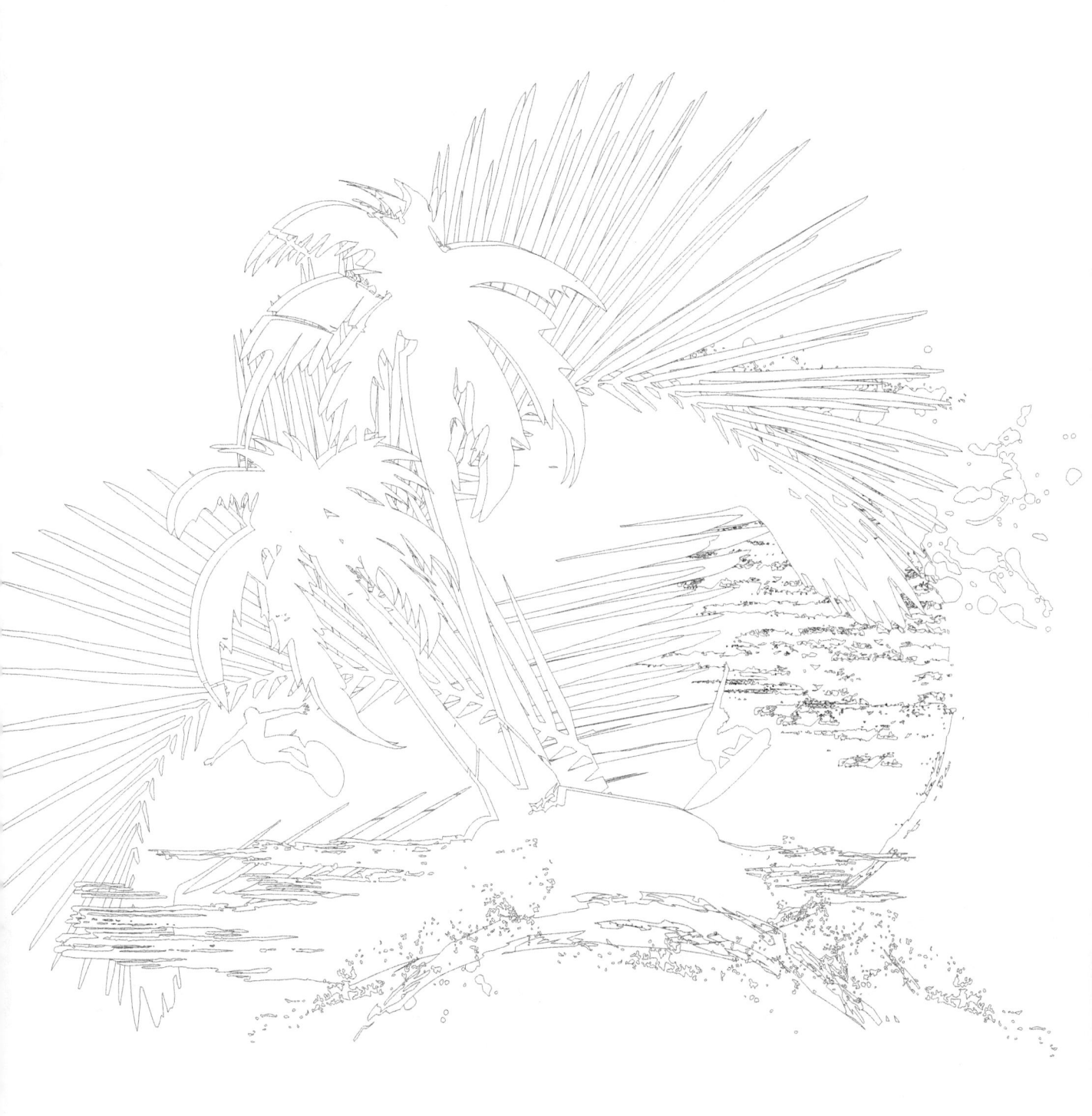

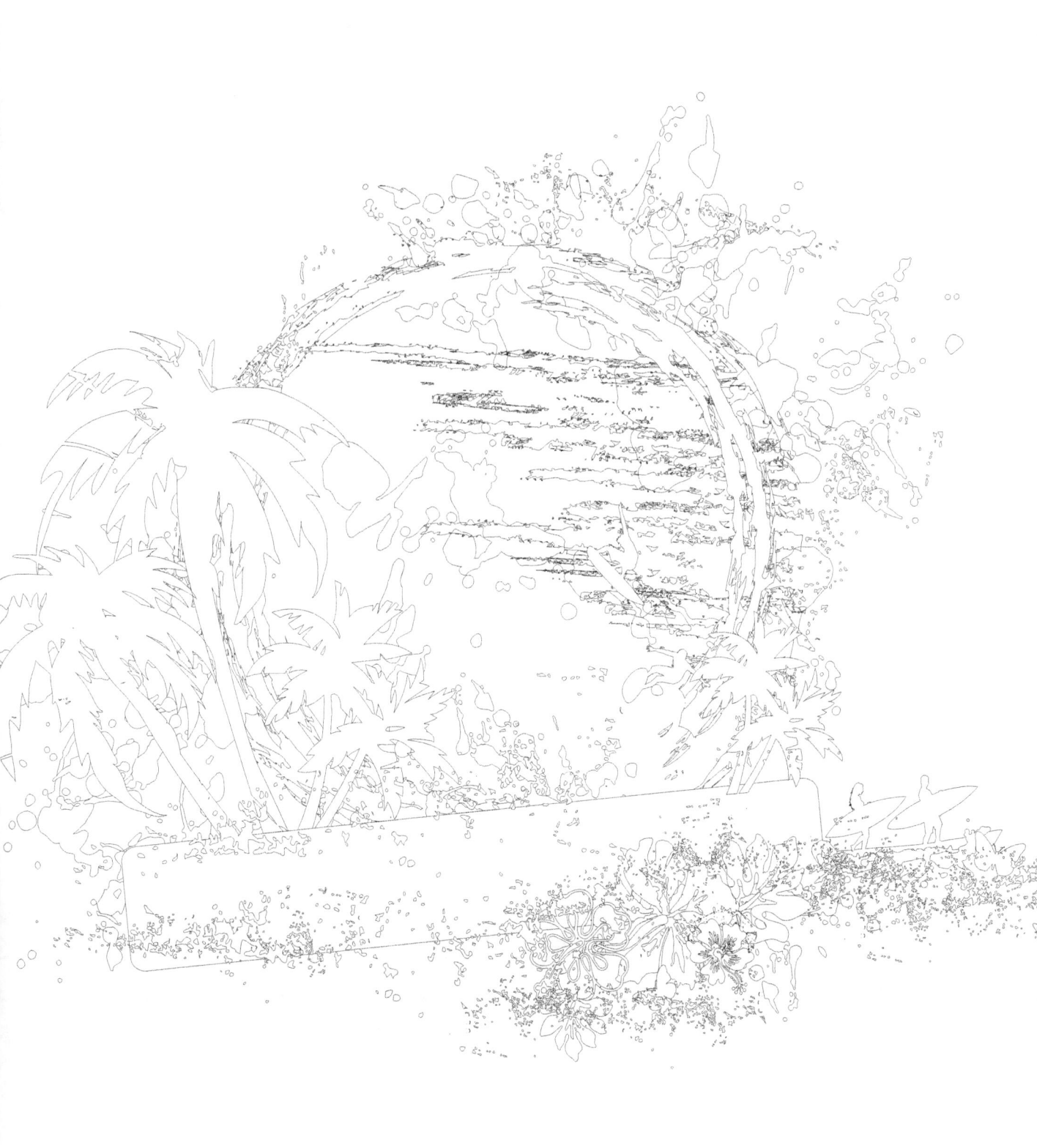

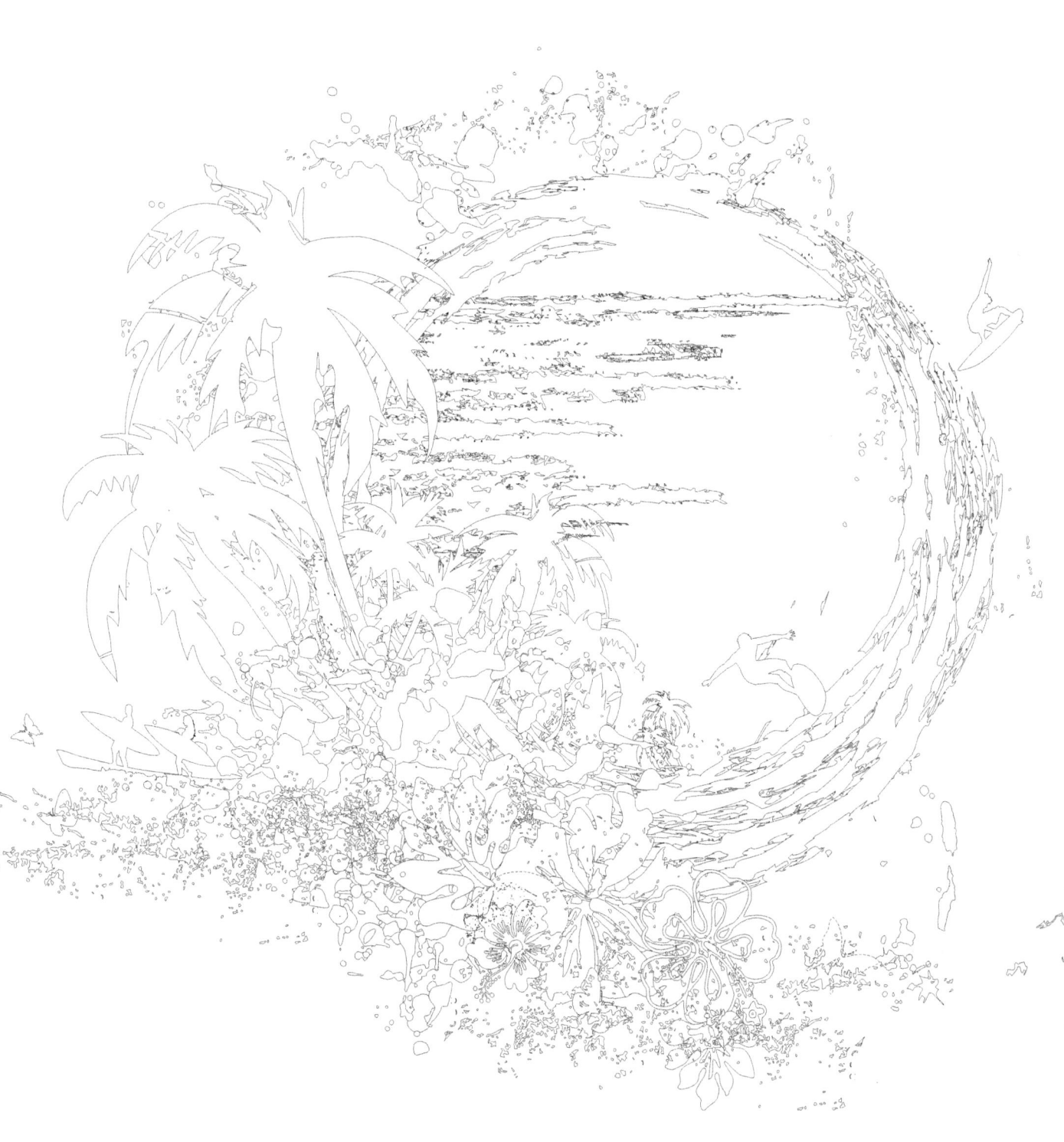

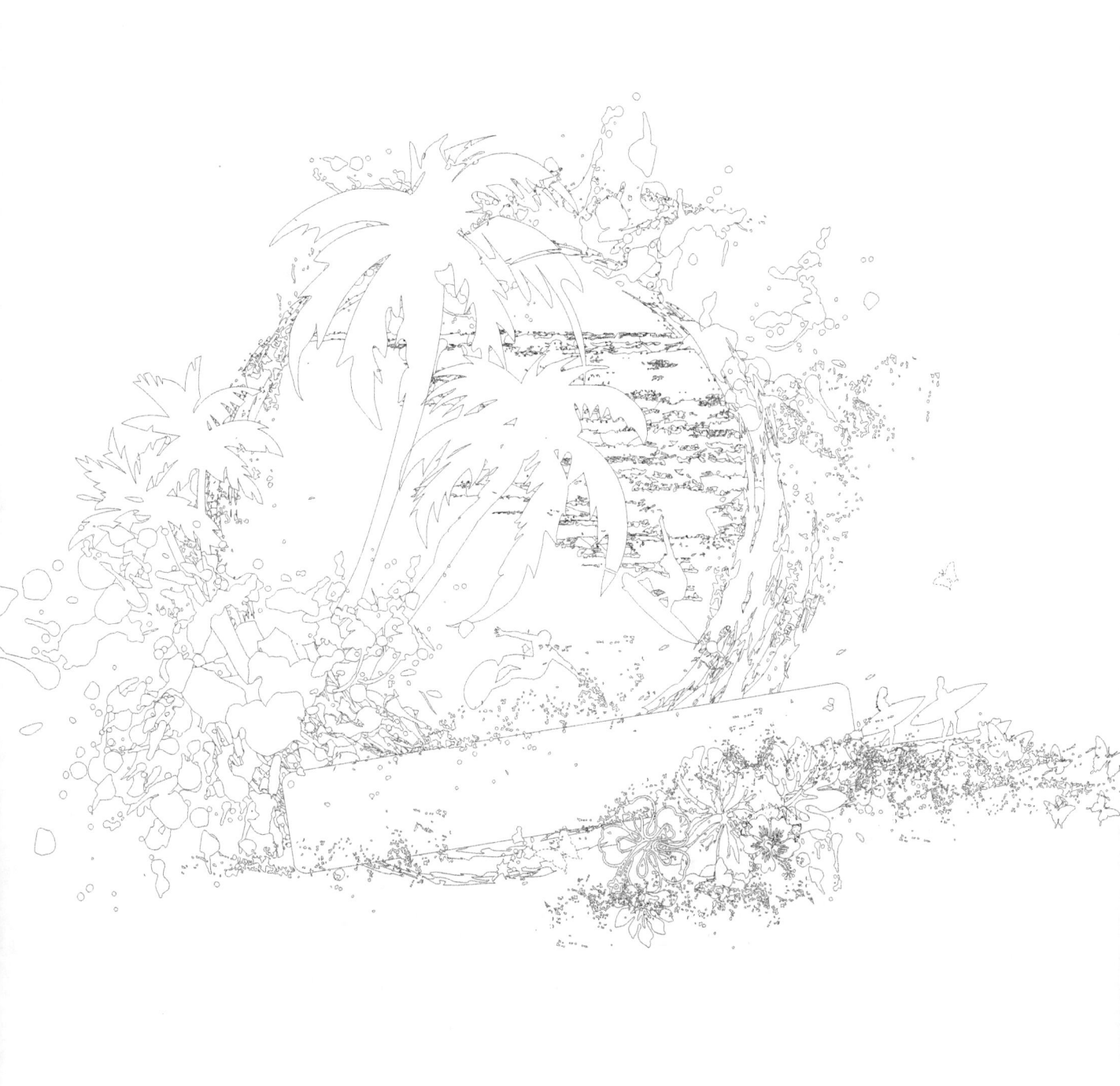

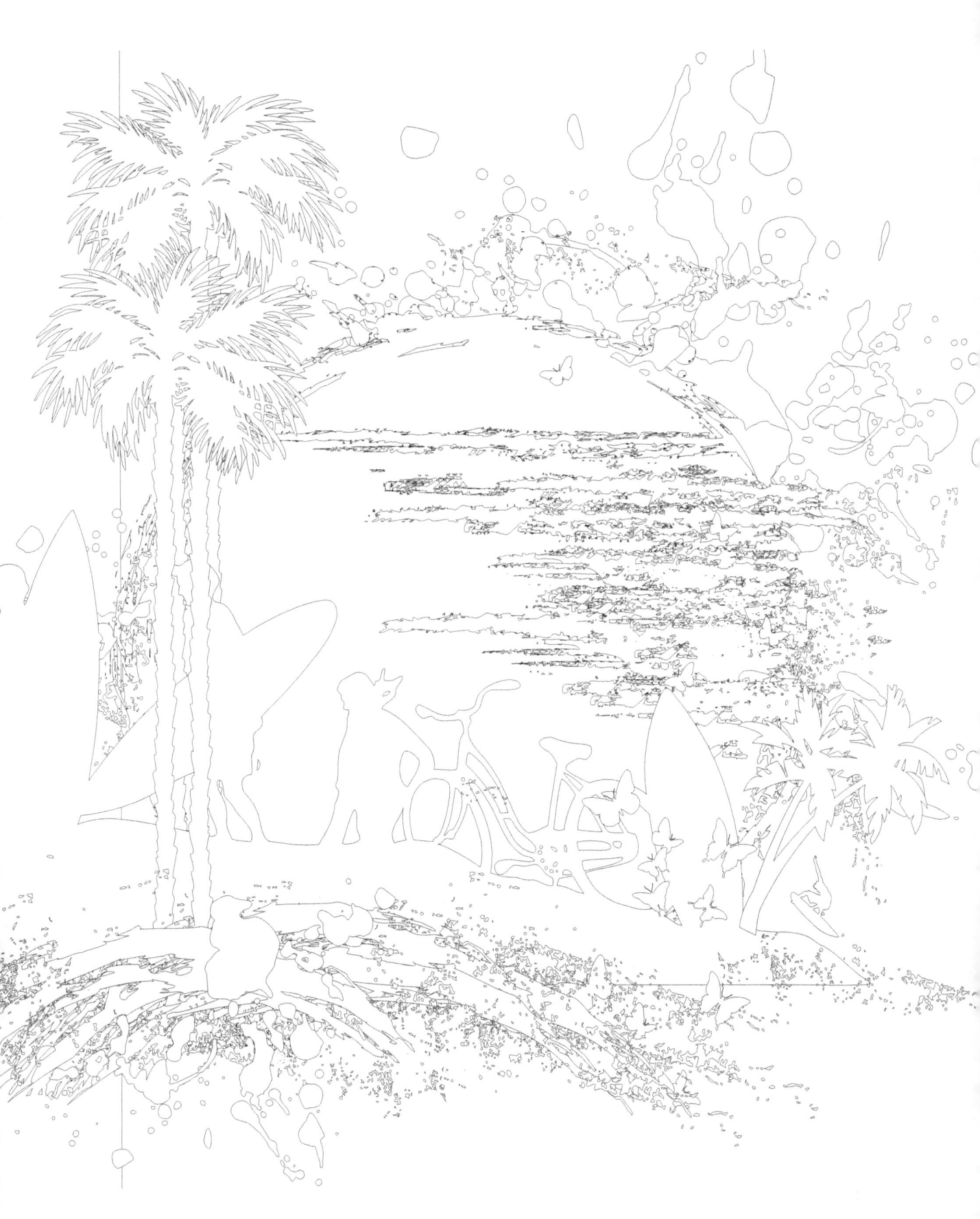

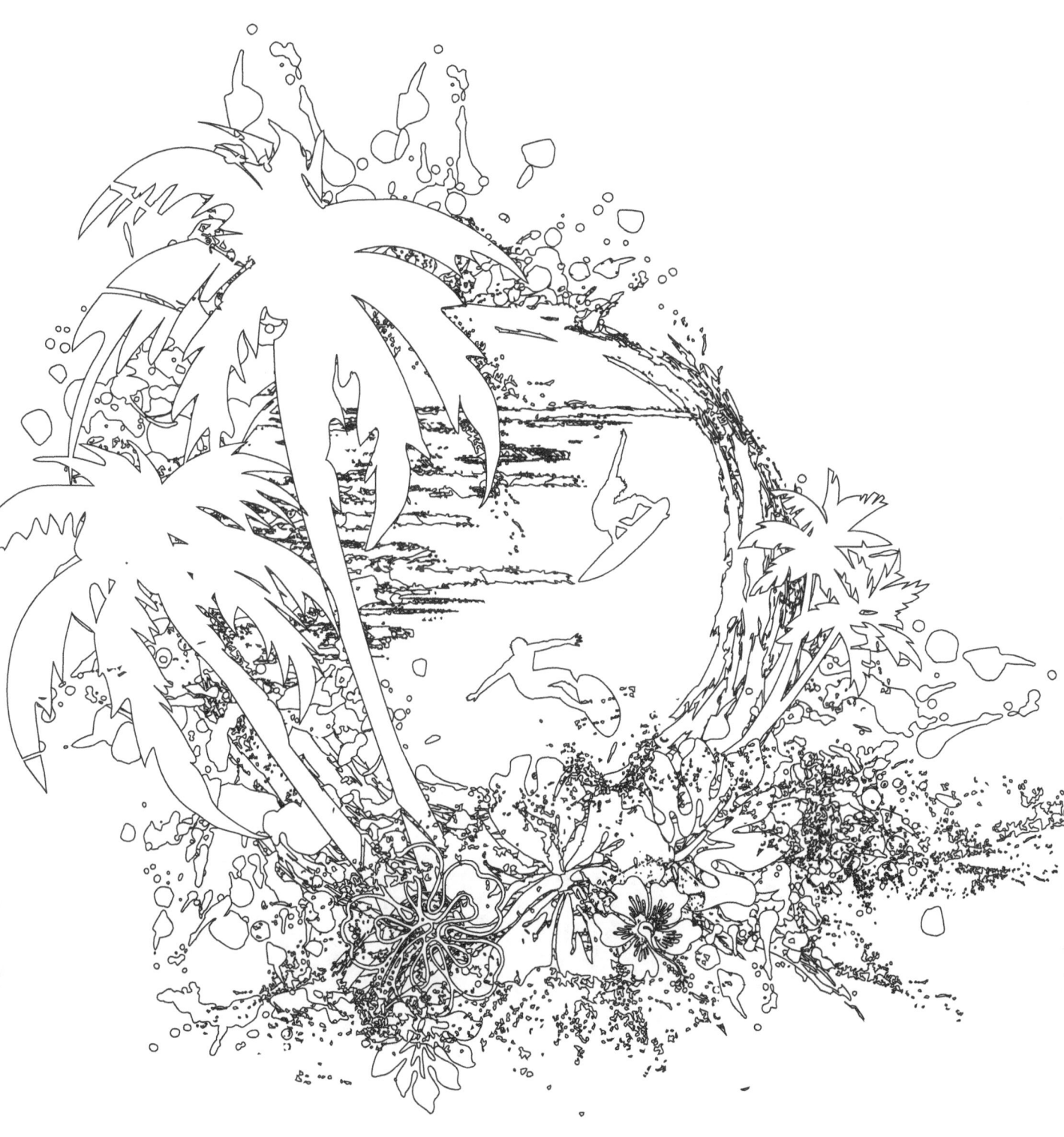

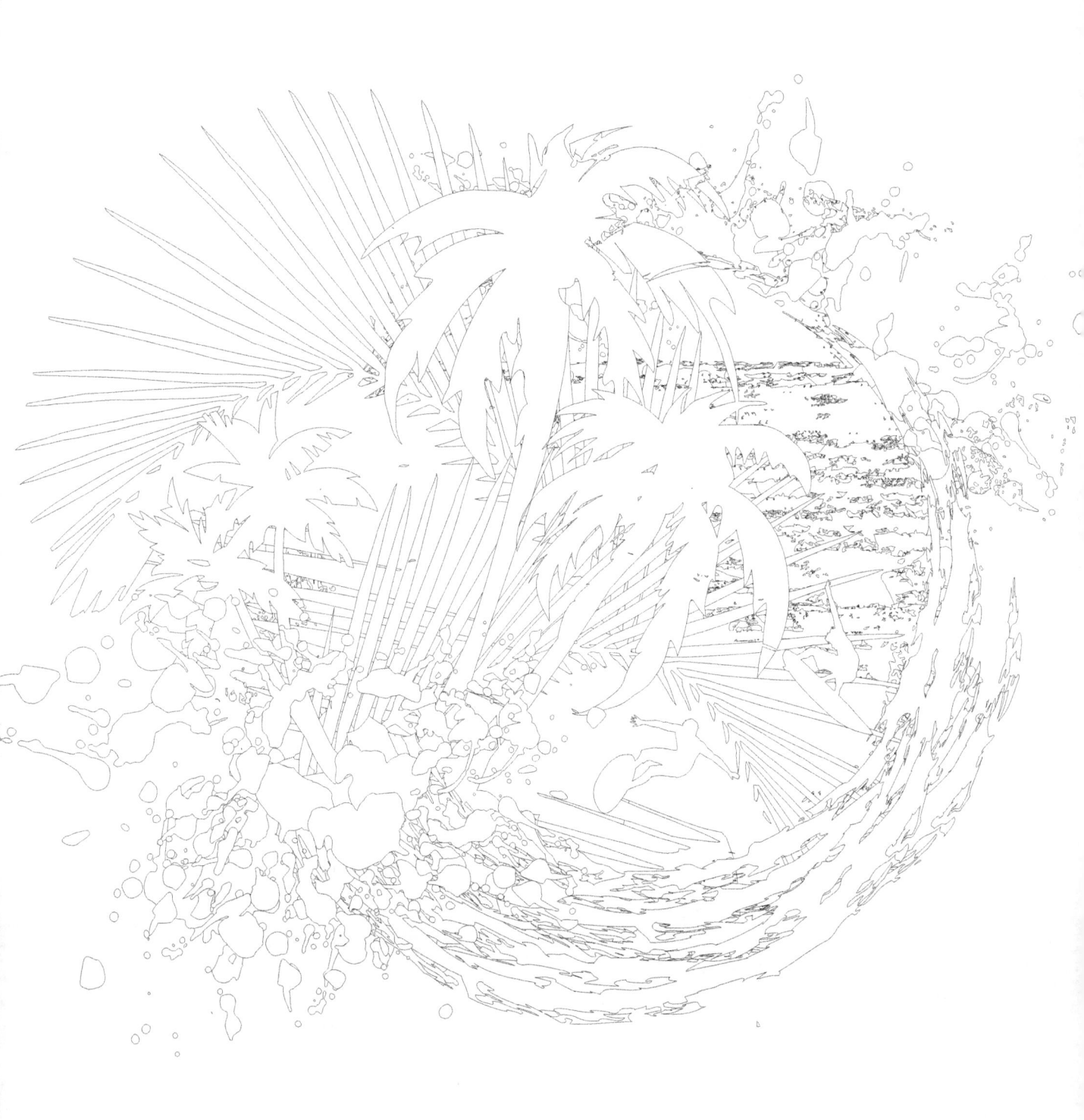

www.ingramcontent.com/pod-product-compliance
Lightning Source LLC
Chambersburg PA
CBHW080648180526
45168CB00008B/3342